LIMBERLOST

¤

Jeanine Stevens

FUTURECYCLE PRESS

www.futurecycle.org

Cover composite by Diane Kistner of a photo by Steve Johnson; author photo by Greg Chalpin; cover and interior book design by Diane Kistner; Gentium Book Basic text and Silom titling

Library of Congress Control Number: 2019937396

Published by FutureCycle Press
Athens, Georgia, USA

ISBN 978-1-942371-71-7

For Gregory and all my family

Contents

III.

IV.

*Extracts from my diary reveal what my memory
cannot revive: the daily dust of my daily life.*

—Simone de Bouvier

I.

Sifting

A Maidu site along the Sacramento River
surrounded by corn and tomato fields.

We grasp wooden trays: back and forth
motion reveals—
      trade beads, fish bones,
pollen grains, like all sorting, winnowing.

We sift, separate what floats to the top.
On small note cards
we identify remains in ink:

      shell bracelet, bone amulet.
Like conversation beyond what is said.
What myth are you giving me, what old story?

What I keep is memory: a worn belt buckle
from gravel beds along the Feather River,
      two silver hearts
detached from a friendship ring, inexpensive
perfume bottle with pansy flower top.

By afternoon, delta breezes coat my face
with rich loam as I continue to rub
earth through metal
      for clues to my old trade routes.

Some particles, like words,
are too distant to catch in this finer mesh.

Acorn

Daylight, dry foothills above Clipper Gap,
leaves scamper through the open door.
I drink deep draughts of cedar, a hint of resin,
        sit down to write.

On my desk, you leave a plump
green acorn held together
by speckled, sage-colored leaves.

It stays until the first snow flurries move
the oak forest behind my window,
        then turns brown,
a glazed patina like an expensive piece
of Bakelite jewelry, a chameleon blending
into deep, rich, wood grain.

        The wobbling cylinder
begins to move, shudder, change position.
With my pen, I nudge it over.
A small larva, white as milk, tumbles, twists,
gyrates and hatches
        early in the warm room,
a tiny pinhole perfectly carved—the exit point.

I hold the acorn, a smooth fire-hardened
aboriginal spear, your quiet strength,
place it on our pillow and call it foreplay.

Our Room with Open Door

The Dordogne 2004

At Hôtel Les Glycines, sunlight sprinkles on rush mats,
high ceilings are restored to look old. Arches
and roses stretch for acres. Most of the afternoon,
poets sit by the far pond writing or napping. Then,
Kir on the terrace, a late dinner of *foie gras,*
poisson grillé, and *tarte aux pommes.* The full moon
basks over the green Vézère River, where small
broad-backed horses drank their fill. Their delicate
skulls now sit in the museum; it is said their fur
was pale yellow to bluish gray. I'd love to see
tiny hooves kicking up colored stones at river's edge.
Soft voices in canoes hold torches for an evening journey.
In the morning, flat faces of lime-scented geraniums
press against our window, insistent, damp and warm.

Black Figs

Like a gypsy king, the smithy presided
over his anvil, told raunchy jokes.
His permanent scowl kept girls
    just outside the door.

Skin blackened and cracked
like his leather apron,
there was something honest
about the smell of horse, sweat, tobacco.

Other men surrounded him. Pungent,
smoldering oak,
tangy juices from spittoons,

    the aroma mixed
with hides, reds and yellows,
an ancient rub:
    cumin, black figs and honey.

A Date at the La Brea Tar Pits

In early evening, we stood next
to dilapidated fences guarding
black pools. Huge plaster replicas
    hovered—
sculptures at their dusk.

Tar smell, heavy and dense, oozed.
Fat bubbles glistened,
reflected scant daylight—
    a false haven
for birds and eager beasts.

He wanted to kiss me,
but it didn't seem right, there
    at the edge
of the Pleistocene,
    at the edge of time.

Now, a lab covers the pits.
Technicians behind glass
examine glossy bones permanently
trapped—
    no dew-laced lip prints,
not even a faint impression.

First Love

From kissing you, I learn chemistry,
a mix of cocktail sauce and lemon.

We eat jumbo shrimp, walk the pier,
never tire of "Slaughter on 10th Avenue."

A summer of Pacific sun, baby oil,
salt spray and the bright green sea.

I didn't know the Winter Formal
        would be our last time
and "Blue Tango" our last dance.

I didn't know I would find
the same salt and sweet sweat
with another.

        We only thought about hunting
grunion in a stark black night—
the only light
        a cigarette red across the bay.

Catching the Last Métro

After Simone de Beauvoir

You come to a point where daily life
      has its limits—

Paris I mean, man-made housekeeping,
      pots and pans, streetlights.

Preferable, the solitude of islands
on old maps, a jutting promontory, say Gibraltar,
      between two oceans.

Often, I enjoy one gin fizz at the Jockey Club,
      held tight in the arms of men, the urgency

of here and now, warmth of strange hands,
      fake love; settings of illicit bars a comfort.

Raised with caution, I manage a last drink
at Place de la Bastille, or the pinball
saloon on Avenue de Clichy,
      always in time to catch the last Métro.

Bolder, I welcome pickups on the streets;
      cars follow my bare legs and spiked heels.

Tonight, it's a young thug with a long
scar on his pink cheek and a pointed, pimply chin.
      His friend buys us coffee.

Late, I hop on the platform, don't know if he
will strike me or kiss me.
      I let him have the 20 francs.

Assemblage

I could spend a lifetime on Cornell's
wild dolls or wood balls in an empty box:
blue space, rectangles,
thumbprint labyrinth.

If I opened a childhood drawer,
I might find a gray rabbit's foot,
two silver hearts joined, a membership card
for Camp Fire Girls—
someone who is lucky in love
and worships flames.

On our trips to museums, my brother
recalls the artillery and shrunken heads.
For me, it's the power of Indiana limestone,
the neatly scribed notations on display cases
and, in winter, the tamale man
pushing his steaming cart through the snow.

On the floor near my chair, other stimuli
flutter, a memory trace, a lone feather.
A soul forgotten?
Is it any one thing
that splinters the glass door?

All Degrees of White

Decision starts in first grade,
snow hugging trunks,
    trees barely visible.

We each receive a clear sheet, not the acrid
spongy manila, but pure white smelling of ice,
    a blue or black crayon:
no suggestions, no directions.

No sound except roman numerals ticking,
a clanking water heater wakened
by wet mittens,
and the smell of warm wax
    in small hands.

Some begin right away: a dark glove,
wild parrots, wavy amoebic flakes, rigid
smokestacks, a lump of coal
with sticks for eyes. Others tear paper,
    create jagged waterfalls.

I think about small animals
in hiding,
    choose blue.
My furry rabbit feet travel
diagonally, disappear top right.

Rabbits

We live in a small rental, like a duplex, but we call it
a double. Plain with no grass, we use old tablespoons to
dig in the ground. The neighbor kid eats dirt while my
brother and I use our spoons to dig trenches for beetles
and ants. I am five; it is early winter, no snow on the
ground. Father and uncles are just home from rabbit hunting.
The doleful things line up, side by side, on the kitchen floor,
maybe eight or twelve...the whole room is full of rabbits.
Newspapers are spread beneath to catch the blood leaking
onto the worn, greenish linoleum. The skinning begins:
crunching, tearing, ripping—sounds of separation. I think
"These rabbits will never be whole again!" It goes slowly,
blood is starting to mat on the gray, brown, and white fir.
I remember the song about a daddy who went a hunting
to get a rabbit skin, to make a bunting, to wrap the little
baby in, and hoped these pelts were not going to be my
winter coat. The whole house is hot from the wood stove,
but I feel chilly. A strong odor, wild and unfamiliar,
is not offensive. Finally, the slaughter is over! Newspapers
are rolled up with the innards inside. One rabbit is chopped
into pieces and fried up for supper with creamy white gravy
and potatoes mashed with Borden's canned milk. A thigh
is darkened with blood. Father says, "I will take that one,"
spitting the buckshot onto his tin plate.

Wild Asparagus

At the farm in Michigan, Mother sits in a wicker chair
cleaning wild asparagus for soup and fritters.

Late Depression, breadlines snake around corners,
but my parents get married anyway, and usually
kill and stew up an old hen for Sunday dinner.

She could have been a vegetarian, loved spring peas
right from the pod and leftover corn-on-the-cob.

I want to hide under the bed from Philco's green eye
that doesn't lie, that foretells of a rougher decade to come:

> factories waiting...
> lines remaining, men still standing...
> boots wet with foreign mud.

We move to the city. Dad works swing shift,
some new kind of aircraft.

We don't know we will walk to school
under protective custody

or about food rationing, haven't yet heard
those romantic-sounding names:
The Solomons, Tarawa, The Royal Hawaiian Hotel.

Sugarloaf

In fourth grade, the teacher was evil,
placed columns of math problems
on our desks, even before the bell rang!
By 9 A.M., I was defeated
and still three hours until lunch.

Anemic, no snack breaks,
by 11 A.M., weak,
then Geography, a photo,
the lofty mountain in Brazil: Pão de Açúcar.
Named for the refined sugar packed
in bread-like loaves,
it towered above Rio de Janeiro.
I could smell Sugarloaf baking,
crust cracking cinnamon,
coated in confectioner's sugar.

It held me until the walk home at noon
for leftovers, and a small helping
of pink watery junket. If we had enough
dime-sized food tokens (red = meat),
lunch was bologna on fluffy Wonder Bread
and bright cherry Kool-Aid.

We returned to rest our heads on desks;
a symphony played over the loudspeaker.
Part of the afternoon, we knitted
squares for blankets, our soldiers freezing,
hungry in a distant European winter.

The Weekly Reader

Fridays were good—they meant
Saturday matinees, baby sitters, burgers
and my parents dancing at the Indiana Roof Ballroom.

After lunch, The Weekly Reader
appeared on our desks,
the type in narrow columns,
a treat designed by well-meaning educators,
a diversion from food rationing and air-raid drills.

There were stories about the Liberty Bell,
the invention of the auto, and a few jokes
    —pale ink on dull newsprint.
We became sleepy; boys picked mosquito bites.

In the afternoon, *Life* came in the mail.
I scoured the pages: gray tanks, warplanes, fat bombs,
injuries, bandages, and one

chubby toddler in her green jade jacket,
warm pants and cloth slippers on the steps
of a demolished temple
    —no wound showing.

In color, the shiny paper made war seem
real. But most photos were black and white.

Reading a Used Book in July

I relax into the lawn chair,
open *Fifty Years of American Poetry*
from the free-bin at the local library.
This little Dell paperback is so old, the spine cracks,
the glue disintegrates, and pages fall away
to poems that must have been someone's favorites.

I doze, then wake to words:
    lustful, fickle, elegiac and *spellbinding.*

We come to the mountains for a few quiet days,
too early for the crimson kokanee to spawn.
Perhaps I will write about Canada geese,
lichen, even graffiti.
      Someone painted
the name Neva on fences and granite outcrops.
      We wonder about Neva.

At the Chinese Buffet,
a gnawed bone lay in the dirt planter,
not even a token plastic flower.
      Not good for business.

Here are some lines:
    a Swedish pool boy,
    a patchwork scrap bag,
    a receipt for nail polish from Monoprix.

The sun slips behind the summit.
I put root vegetables in the steamer, realize
I've left my rock cod too long on the sideboard.
You fiddle with the new antenna,
try to get the Summer Olympics from Reno TV.

A page breaks loose, lands on the fish.
Why write unless you praise the sacred places,
     a line now wet and glutinous.
Later a cleansing swim in the lake.

Declaration

I believe in getting up early,
Kurt Vonnegut's advice
about sunscreen and dental floss.
I believe the sexiest part
of a man is the inner thigh,
high up, just where
skin begins to change color. I
believe in trees, the way
they survive on their own terms,
in clay or on the unexpected
side of a hill. I believe
in a woman's right to wear
sultry toenail polish,
to carve the salmon tattoo
on her right ankle.
I still love Lee J. Cobb
and Farley Granger but believe
I am newly excited by Edward Norton
and Matthew Macfadyen.
I believe in friendship, that fire
laid in the depths of winter:
stews, soups and Greek chicken
delivered to my door. I believe
in new love at any age,
the placement of a single flower
on a worn pillow. I believe
in compost—all kinds
of shavings: coffee grounds,
rejected poems. I believe in
home remedies and drip systems.

Herring

Kippers, sardines and anchovies are laid out uniformly
in rectangular tins. Herring, tightly packed in *Lasco* jars,

contort to lumps that appear perfect. Crammed into
a tiny space, each nudges, conforms to its neighbor;

little toes cramped in tight shoes. There is so much
artsy-craftsy in their individual hides, a nudist colony

filled to capacity! Glistening chunks huddle, spoon backs
and stomachs like lovers after a full meal, their salty meat

full and plump with vinegar. When served, they must be
coaxed from the jar with a fancy pickle fork, jiggled onto

the serving plate. Then, herring relax, lose individuality
but remain appetizing in platinum skin. If not eaten, fleshy

sides droop like defeated angel wings. Black peppercorns
as errant eyes escape, jet pupils looking for sour brine.

Dungeness

At the wharf,
we bought two large, cooked crabs,
sunset-orange shells with smears of red.
Carried to the picnic area on the beach,
we sat at a worn table, each immediately
grabbing a claw, pulling out triangles
of sweetness. Our lips turned oily
from butter that began in our mouths then slathered
down arms, so slick we could hardly hold
the bottle of chilled Chardonnay.
Salt spray softened the sourdough bread we tore
into chunks, as if we had never eaten—
as if this was our first meal on earth.
We moved on to the meaty bodies, fringed
membranes no barrier. Fingers were pink
and raw with small cuts from sharp shards.
Hesitating, much as an animal looks
up from his kill, I closed my eyes, heard
the sea wall whisper, tasted
the Pacific on my tongue. You cut the lemon
in half; juice spattered my face. Startled,
I decided I loved the word *crustacean,*
then noticed a warning sign: Lyme Disease.
Too busy to care, not even time for a photo.
Day darkened, sopped paper plates
collapsed. The last fragment finished,
jeweled remnants piled in our wake.

Three about Ecstasy

1.

Strangers in no hurry, just down from *Echo Summit*,
we stop on the left of the highway, park and walk to where
meadow backs up to forest. Sun is new and the cool breeze
lifts branches of dark tamaracks. Bands of corn lily
and monkey flower grow close to the ground. We find
ourselves waist-deep in cream-colored grass and tall,
coarse cinquefoil. At meadow pools, mayflies bask
on rush branches. All at once flurries of white butterflies
settle on tips of the strongest stems. In a vortex we drop
among nettles and other scratchy things, *not caring about
cars in the distance.* It must have been the mile-high elevation.
We lay there, breathless...changed.

2.

Snow obscures broken fences and closed motels. Pilings under
the dock at Ehrman Mansion leak icicles, thick and pendulous
in a slow melt. I kneel on dark sand, touch water, slate blue and
frothy. Later, thinking of Whitman, I clip the last of the lavender
lilacs by the back door and place them in a pitcher on the table.
The green heart-shaped leaves ruffle and tenderly hold scented
spikes. We missed the white one this year, rare and not always
predictable. Later, in a full moon, we sleep on and off, tangle
in and out of sheets...get up three times to rearrange the
soft muslin quilt and fluff pillows. You doze. I wake early—
Surprise! the press of the white lilac against the window,
sweet, wet, and wanting.

3.

We begin our hike, Tahoe Rim at Spooner Summit Trailhead.
The title is a little off-putting for romance, and the climb suddenly
steeper than I like. I follow, watch your hips and thighs move.
I think of cedar planks, the strength of trees, and the aboriginal
space we intrude upon. The trail is slippery with slick pine needles.

We stop in a brief wedge of shade. You don't speak, but pull me through the forest. Fleshy spikes of crimson snow plant poke up through musky earth. Reddish scales curl back to expose bell-shaped corollas, lobes arching over tight leaves. I knock the largest with my boot. We bend down to where moist seeds emerge, tumble and spill into my arms.

House Special

Crossing Nevada's purple hills,
    I pass Garnet Mountain,
where folks with small hammers
chunk out dusty red stones.

A few miles west, I stop
at the "Oldest Hotel in Nevada,"
order the *SPECIAL*—
sort of a "House Chow Mein."

The first inch or so is tasty, but salty,
heavy on canned bean sprouts.

    My fork lifts, exposes
a plump blue blowfly. I refuse
a replacement, order black coffee,
then notice the kitchen door ajar,
    dry desert breezes
cooling off the cook.

II.

Snowshoe in Summer

In this high desert,
we find the marker tight
against the base of the Sierras.

Modest, the stone stands alone,
perfect for one who loved solitude.

Snowshoe Thompson. Age 49 Years
Born 1827 Telemark, Norway
Died 1876 Carson Valley, Nevada

The next purpling range ripples on heat waves.
He loved to hear the colors move.

At my feet,
between sagebrush and sand,
a garter snake wriggles around boulders,
brings his own
      gold stripe and small bones.

Near the road,
a scrawny mule deer
startles away from the green
of a new golf course.

We look back; in the white noonday sun,
Thompson's headstone glistens alabaster,
the cross made of long distance skis—
      etched deep.

Genoa, Nevada

Mind of the Glacier

Six A.M., overcast along the Icy Straits, the water
clouded with milky floes, fragments of a lost language?

Destruction, debris, rubble dropped on a whim.
I remember the Tlingit mask, a tiny face
        emerging from one cheek screaming.

Approaching the inlet, we enter a calm bay
almost devoid of color, azure vaults
hoarding all the hues and shadows.

Glacial advance, ground-down evidence,
dwellings shoved into the sea.

All talk at the ship's railing is cameras,
magnification, and who is standing
        in the way of the best shot.

Pulling away, iceblink from a faraway field
gleams yellow. The rigid tundra stands watch,
stunted growth hiding footsteps.

Splitting corridors, ancient migration routes from Asia
reach south to Nevada's Great Basin,
amorphous space, a land we used to know.

Here, old words survive. *Athabaskan,*
leaving behind—
        Raven, the little god who stole the sun.

Hoarfrost (*Gelée blanche*)

—Camille Pissarro

With stout walking staff, the farmer trudges
uphill, bent with his bundle
of kindling for the evening fire.
Absent willows climb in a late afternoon,
upper branches invisible
over a far ridge. Shadows bend
with the terrain, foliated in winter haze.
Opaque glare sheets a white glaze
over purple-ribboned furrows.
How intriguing to add swatches
of slick hoarfrost, like a patchwork
clipped and laid in place
on carefully tilled earth, his *Snow Effect.*
At the bottom of the swale,
I imagine the artist just out of frame,
warm brazier and small stool
under his gray umbrella. Pungent
waste rags with too much color
scatter and stiffen.
He is excited by the cartilage
of this new work: arc lines, delicate clavicles.
As his outer mood directs bones
of the landscape, the inner explores
the beauty of absence.
I don't agree with the critic who says
an entire grove is missing.
Notice a suggestion of Pollarded trees
lining the stream, reaching trunks
made even more willowy
by the earth's curvature, the entire piece
a caged windbreak.
A small shrub dissolves into flaming
garnet clumps. The walker
continues, soft crush of ice underfoot.
All is metered,
slow stride in tomorrow's sun.

Oblique

So pleased to be out early,
the young mother in brisk winter sun
wears her new white gloves.

She pins fresh laundry,
prefers the makeshift clothesline,
the wood pegs that gently
hold her little boy's shirts,
not like spring-pins
      that crimp delicate fabrics.

She wonders if grazing deer
she saw yesterday notice
the smoky fragrance of autumn leaves.

Her hands reach up with the last
bedsheet...bright and quick.

With his expensive scope,
the hunter is certain
he sees white scut,
      spots
the white flag
      for a clean shot.

No one is charged.

The husband in grief takes his sons
away from the changeable forest
to a prairie where light and shadow
are what they seem,

where folks are accountable, and no one
mistakes
a buffalo for a locomotive.

Cartographer

In my next life, globes will be obsolete.
I will be a mapmaker and superimpose

green climate changes over blood red
political borders, place black vertical

columns around suspected oil reserves,
and use five dimensional images to highlight

prehistoric game trails. This will be my
calling, my vocation. I will amble from door

to door, hawking my ancient broadside—
a satellite photo—the polar ice cap,

a hole the size of Indiana. Belatedly,
I leave tattered flyers on rundown doorsteps.

Tincture

She selects a prompt
from assorted items: small votive,
unscented, linen white,
    new and untouched.

So like the small urn by her bedside,
not a humidifier but a black plastic base
with a metal cup on top.
    Electric.

The tincture placed inside
had a spicy, syrupy odor meant to cure coughs.
She rolled over, face down,
    into the boiling liquid.

The babysitter phoned
the Melody Inn, a local tavern
where her folks had gone for Tom Collins
after two weeks nursing sick children.

Just seven, in pain,
she dialed her grandfather,
got him out of bed.
Dressed in his three-piece suit,
he arrived before her parents.

She never scarred, knew he could cure anything,
better than chants, balms or alchemy.

Later today, picking up a pricey marinade
from Italy, she recognizes the scent
    —balsam.

Main Street

A big shop with heavy machinery
for refitting soles. Repaired shoes, snug
in paper sacks fastened with name tags
like the ones hooked to coats of immigrants.
On the wall, a photo, marchers
dressed in white robes and pointed hats
carry burning torches.
At the corner drugs, I stop
for a thick vanilla cone.
Most family are now gone, except
a third cousin who runs a small antique shop.
I buy a doll, not expensive; the sun
has turned one leg from flesh to milky white.
She has a blue knit coat
and a fluffy fur for cold winters.
I grab lunch at the take-away counter,
fly a straight line from Chicago to Dallas.
Fractured clouds appear volcanic
in a blinding afternoon. Out my window
the jet's smutty bolts,
both gray and shiny, do their job.
Something in my visible spectrum allows
a peek in the frame—
marchers line up on the wing,
like a hologram, bright and quivering.
I realize the doll is just my age
when we moved west, a child with legs unformed.
No matter how much time passes,
with any one thing—photo, toy
or nametag—always
another threshold to cross.
I lower the shade.
She rides in an overhead bin,
stiff soles turned up to the sky.

Moonlight

In this aging hotel, jittery gaslight
plagues the long-term resident.
Munch etched a shadowy mass
except for the transparent triangle
holding his chin.

      Leery of this night, legs
tuck under a cold bench; he does not want
to disturb the determined funnel
stretching a white finger
      down the long hallway.

The startled moon—amok—
stains the lumpy sofa, feverishly
polishes a pewter hurricane.

Waiting alone for so long, his hair
      turns alabaster.

      What is more infectious,

this tunnel of blackness
or the blinding red chandelier
crackling midnight air?

Does each tarnished prism
hold varied facets,
reflections of all he used to be?

The gray strand on his sleeve
unravels like a paramecium
pricked in a Petri dish.

Pilgrim State

On good days, he minces steps, avoids busted pavers,
carries water in a tin can to the woody red geraniums.

He remembers the metal carts, wheels spinning,
glass bottles rattling, and the young nurse scoring

his head with gentian violet—the incision to sever
thoughts no one else could bear, the mind mapped

for travel. In time, bone chips wandered his corridors;
words picked from a hat cover concave depressions.

Tattered art prints hang askew on flaking walls.
He is the last patient left behind and reads a faded notice:

This Surgery is Illegal!

At dusk, air currents slam doors: a cold room,
an iron bed; the night-light snaps off automatically.

He listens to pigeons speak-speak in rafters.
He is used to odd noises in decrepit buildings.

> *After viewing film archives, Pilgrim State Hospital,*
> *Brentwood, New York*

Mother Mary

I'm certain I was a brat, wanted
to be her favorite young cousin.
This was a family that spent more time
talking at dinner than eating.
In the basement, we dramatized Snow White
and other classics. And so smart,
she had a column in the high school paper.

The initial psychotic episodes were shocking.
We thought she would snap out of it.
I was invited to spend a weekend
just after she turned 19.
Drifting to sleep, she said,
"I know the Virgin Mary is waiting
for me on the roof."
I don't recall her being religious;
I was the churchgoer, helped out in the nursery
on Sundays and sang in the choir.
Was it something about flight,
indecision, forgiveness? In a rush
I followed. We leaned a ladder
against the stone wall.
She was up so fast, then out of sight.

Near midnight, the ocean breeze gave off
a sweet-salt mist and moved
gray fog over the sparse hillside.
I believed her and expected
to see something. By now
the family was out, my aunt standing
to the side, face plain and dark.
My uncle, backed up to the edge
of the yard for a better view.
I remember his striped P.J.'s billowed in the wind,
the sky bright, his eyes resting and wet.
Inky, the dog, ran in circles.

We had no instructions from doctors,
didn't know if we should enter into her visions.
But I remember this family together
trying to understand. I wanted someone
to be waiting up there,
                    someone, anyone.

Hermosa Beach

Because it was summer, we had night beaches, inky and warm.
Lamplights near the breakwater infused surf with gold dust.
With my cousins: we didn't know how brief

That fall, there would be high school,
one who loved the sea stationed aboard the *USS Boxer*
and another drifting off to Camarillo State Hospital.

But this night we dragged gunnysacks to the edge,
waited on sopping sand. Hypnotized
by a gentle tide, fuzz rolled between our toes.
Silver flash—wiggling, twisting,
        egg-laying food source.

Not knowing the moon's trajectory or her plans for the evening,
we rushed, scooped, lost some,
gleaming slits sucked back into the black Pacific.

Grunion knew what they were in for,
predicted their brief future at tide's whim,
eggs already deposited before the next surge.

        We were proud to say,
"We fished without hooks."
Shaped like smelt, the grunion resisted cornmeal,
curled in the popping lard...and were still.

44

November, 2 A.M.

Garlic and onion, the aroma of winter's first stew
permeates the house. I wake
and move through rooms
to one that disappears in daylight hours.

The colors deep, shadows
not completely black,
but ruby warm and vaporous. I stumble
over a wicker basket full of second drafts.

In the curio cabinet, like relics in a museum:
Tarot cards (not mine),
two G.I. Joes complete with jeep,
a ticket stub for *Manon of the Spring*,
a cat made of sawdust and a photo
of me by the creek reading *The Ink Dark Moon*.

My husband's rolling snore, somehow
comforting; the last coals
in the hearth snap apart and rest.

In the dark dawn, the wobbling possum
comes home to sleep under our deck.
Milk bottles rattle on the porch.

How do I begin this day, uncertain how
my life occurred, unable to touch
items I can't remember?
Do we all have hidden rooms as evidence?

The day owl fusses on his branch,
the resident hawk settles in his redwood.

I make coffee and pull a piece of silver
salmon from the freezer for the evening meal.

I think one soldier had a missing hand.

Gremlin

noun. blamed for the disruption
of any procedure

Working on our dissertations,
it is the only rental car we can afford.
But we splurge at Gepetto's,
order the "Monstro Special," a platter of shellfish
every shade of crimson and blue swimming
in golden butter. An afternoon off,
we head to the Everglades in steamy
overcast. I expect romance—
something to write about later.

We drive deep into foliage, mosquitoes thick
on the glass, dull gray hissing things,
"gallon sippers," wanting us.
The day closes, the A/C fails, the romance goes—
not because of the Everglades,
or the battered red Gremlin, or Florida—
but because I want a hot dog from the 7-Eleven.

You won't stop for water or a snack, say
"You are a grown woman, it will spoil your dinner."
Low blood sugar makes me thoughtful.
I notice your jaw set long ago
in that tenement in Chicago, roaches clicking
on the wall, dropping onto your crib—
left alone with a hunger I can never fill.

Omen

On our way to the coast
for a weekend—some quality time.

The country road dusty
and barely traveled, brambles
sag on weary fences;

field mice scamper after summer's
sprung seeds.
  A large heifer
struggles, leg trapped in barbed wire.

Flies already cling to her startled,
seeping eyes. Whites roll
up so far they obliterate pupils.

  You free her.
She lopes away across the meadow.

John Muir hated cows, said they *trashed
the meadows.*

I wonder if the gash
on her leg will heal.
  You're quiet,

say, "I'm tired of disruptions."

On this trip, I realize
we won't be offering sweet apples

to blessed horses.
No petting gallant foreheads.

The Keeping Room

*There was a woman who loved her husband
but couldn't live with him. —D. H. Lawrence*

1.

After years of leaving,
temporary apartments, a rollaway
or sleepsack in a friend's living room,
she bought him a doublewide mobile home,
parked in back of their half acre
in joint custody, furnished with old
wedding gifts: glass percolator,
Franciscan pottery, fondue pot,
Weber BBQ, cherry-clustered tablecloth
no one bothered to iron. Late at night,
peering through her back window,
she didn't expect to find such comfort
in the glowing hobnail lamp
cornered in his room. Sometimes
they didn't speak for a week, then spent
three days together in bed. Afterwards,
mended a fence or shopped at Kroger's.

2.

In spring, she cultivates
a small strip of ground by the gravel walkway:
gourds, squash and pumpkins running
forty feet, a symbolic divider, a keeping room.
She positions herb-filled wine barrels along
a flowering maple hedge. Some mornings
they talk over coffee, pick nibbling insects
and worms. Some afternoons they sit
at the worn picnic table to shell peas
and drink Merlot. In late summer, he slices
pumpkins to stew down and freeze for holiday pies.

3.

By October, she pulls
wine barrels aside. Underneath,
pale, ivory-skinned roots creep
over the gravel barrier, poke above
ground, longish fingers with fleshless tips
that plunge under
then rise like whales breaching,
swimming toward him. She points
the shovel, chops, begins to amputate:
tendons, sinews, cartilage. She hesitates,
remembers *Wake of the Red Witch:*
John Wayne, the ship's anchor cutting
dive tubes, the blue octopus lurking below
spewing black ink. Not wanting to sever
connections, she leaves the roots in place,
exposed to autumn air.

*Keeping Room: in country homes, a buffer between the
elements and the real living area to store drying herbs tied
with raffia, craft projects, and mud-caked boots.*

My Kitchen in California

It's December,
making Marseilles Candlemas Cookies,
I'm caught by the verbs:

Cream: My wooden spoon has a will
of its own, giving up long, languorous strokes.

Beat: until slick and elastic.

Knead: the soft dome on my marble board
seems to stretch, arch under the heel of my palm.

Roll: a firm massage. What pleasure,
the walnut-size lumps finding
their way into sausage shapes.

Slit: the only sharp movement required.

>   If the aroma of a Madeline dipped
>   in fragrant tea reignites Marcel's vision
>   of parlors, sofas, and linens,
>   for me this command recalls
>   the aborigine's ritual surgery with a stone knife.
>   I sharpen mine with trepidation,
>   cleave the full length,
>   careful not to cut too deep.

Cover: Hard not to peek as they puff
and swell, double in size under a warm towel.

Bake: Oblongs emerge like pendulous crystals
hung from chandeliers, deep caverns,
rough but nice to hold.

I *top* with clear sugar chips, *place* on a silver tray,
wrap in star-glazed cellophane, and *tie*
the handle with mauve grosgrain ribbons.

False Pilgrim

—Six for Gertrude Stein

My feet are not quantum
nor measured in brown:
boxes, toggles and bones.

I want more than tossing stones
like vagabond shoes, or something
wild, like snakes on Mars.

Wren catches fortune
in her throat, disturbs
and scatters fake winds.

The arena fills with winter rains.
Each clasp repairs, latches
bronze with clean and shine.

The hastened trek brought me
        here;
my cancelled check keeps me
        near.

The borders of Rome never were,
calculations made in error;
turn around, shoot the arrow.

III.

Imprint

It was a sugar maple near the road—
with blackest trunk
five decades ago—beyond,
just alleyway. Refuse heaps
in bent trash receptacles.
I watched from the door:

    late month. November

mums golden near split cement.
Did the maple, ever, or never,
drop leaves by my late birthday,
not that late month,
after or before? Replacement
    of the spoken—
our aging, our resigning.
Replacement, a snapshot,
restless equinox. Now

    I recognize this place,

the part the maple played from summer
to winter, given
as a small voice, like the organ
rising from old North Church.
Roads. Sounds of river clams, dark wet.

    Should I record imprints?

Now I see clearly: seasons,
early years, residue
of reconstructed thought.
In the alleyway, the rusty tin
tilts on its side,
retrieved for a last swift kick.

V Shapes against Blue

In this withering light
three slender oaks expose
their imperfections, do not ask
to be noticed. Like Macbeth's hags,
they intertwine
spindly branches in dry mud.

Unashamed, they flaunt
warts, cankers, black galls full of fungi.
Pests suck sage-colored limbs,
knobs disfigure brittle ribs.
Yet they accept,
even tolerate, my looking.

Their upper limbs toss
so many V shapes against blue.
I want to think violet
or vermilion, hues that belong below ground
where glassy bugs
gnaw, rearrange roots. I want
a side view: a slice of earth
to see pink worms
and purple voles digging new channels.

Come spring, I don't know
if they will sprout
lime-colored leaves graced
with golden finches. These woods seem
an unbreathing place:
birds are barely here; their songs
elude me. I grow even
paler in winter's deep shade.

Invisible

The day I became
invisible, I walked
into a small photo
shop, rang a bell
for service, and no one
came. I stopped
to visit a colleague
on campus; students
swarmed around him.
I slipped out unnoticed.
Through glass, I saw
a friend engrossed
in a meeting. I left
with a cup of water
from the cooler,
then wandered
to a park, watched
ducks. An older
woman also sat,
bent; a spot of blood,
the size of a nickel,
seeped from her arm.
 "I'm not hurt, just
old. My skin breaks
easily." I tiptoed
at the edge of things,
anonymous. It was
somehow peaceful.

Limberlost

Walking into this historic site, house on the left,
garden and woodland to the right—
a poet's home: brown timbers,
a porch and hearth, wavy window glass
and a small shelf
where books can be purchased.

No one lives here now: seams go unstitched;
lentils grow cold on the stove.
The swamp beyond
once stretched to the Potomac.

I try to imagine this place, hot and wet,
Northeastern Indiana
popping seeds,
the flash of silver-netted wings

—blue-green dragonflies singing,
and the sweet splash of amphibians
etching circles near the bank.

In sunny areas, chartreuse pollen floats
like chunks of bright-colored bread,
leaking a cruciferous odor,

and footsteps, the soft press of feet—
what we call prairie chickens.

On my lips, I taste the moisture of salt weed,
dig toes in warm mud below the water table,
and touch the bones of mammoths.

Day Moon Watching

A crow in the small field
pokes white clover, the only snow

in all this deep green. Looking
for worms, tail feathers bob

like a well-oiled tin toy. In the gutter,
a dead squirrel makes a C shape:

scruffy fur, dull eyes, snaggled teeth,
black toes pointing—everything

hideous about a squirrel. The feral cat
moves deliberately toward the road,

ignores the squawking. The rainbird
sprays silvery pellets. The crow

watches, head jerking upward,
throat exposed; surveys the day moon,

attempts to grasp a solitary
white bead in its glistening eye.

Moon Vibrations

—Jackson Pollock

Chicken's eye, jittery cockscomb,
shades of milk, butter and blood,
Over a black crevice, sea snakes
open vents to the underworld.
Fabric unravels, exposes
a ruffled clown,
a Barnum & Bailey universe.
Seen from earth, the spliced moon trips
along a cardboard sky.
If Pollock actually painted
the surface with sulfuric acid (more
white space, silver or pearl),
and if the caverns
were saturated with deep dark pigment
laid down by a brush
made from hooked talons, and if
the fluffy white streaks
actually resembled
the Leghorn rooster's peck and wobble,
I could believe these vibrations.
But this is not
my moon;
Pollock's maneuvers,
not mine.
It is said he loved New York cheddar.
Was he was just hungry
for scrambled eggs? Catsup on the side?

Canyon with Crows

—Georgia O'Keefe

Eggshell sky vacant
except for two crows,
who bring their own words.

Chaparral fuzz like inkblots on a slant,
smaller shrubs are French knots
embroidered in silken thread.
Trees puff and smoke
in an orderly fashion, as if crows
tatted and stitched these hills.
Paint spatters like whispers
through a straw:
sponged charcoal,
color wash, flash flood smudge.

Moisture collects in low creases,
soft folds in an old face
where underground streams are blue.
Birds know better,
think *arroyo.*
Depth catches the mauve eye.
They choose to stay in the sky,
loft in this dry August sun.

I have no choice but to hang
all my thoughts of canyon on this canyon
(a deliberate camouflage not found
on any aerial map).
The longer I look, trees seep;
an old desk blotter obscures notes written
long ago. In my afterimage,
only black lace and fire remain.

The Celadon Bird

Early morning walk at Monument Circle.
Few sounds, horse and carriage at rest.

A tiny bird sits on the dark pavement,

only 4 inches

a striking shade like rich damask.

His eyes close. I consider nudging

feathers stilled

with my camera but fear he may topple.

never stirred

A clear and bright day, but mist to him,
so quiet with opaque lids. So still,

the end of days

like a meditation, not moving this small
celadon heart. Feathers, a brilliance that could
be found in a jungle. Maybe a warbler up

from Tennessee. I think he may be dying.

no winter song

He will not run back and forth like a sandpiper.

He does not move, just thinking:

unaware of danger

nothing, nothing, nothing.

No glance anywhere; I do not want
to leave him, but I, a traveler,
have no soft tree or gentle lilac for rescue.

bower

As I watch, one eye opens to a minuscule
jet bead. Is this his last look?

What does he see? Shiny Florsheims
clicking along or the flower cart's
red wheels running round and round?

I have no further thought and walk on.
Later, I return at half past four

from lunch at the grand Athenaeum

cycle

and a visit to the Vonnegut Memorial Library.

Autumn sun intersects just enough to grace
the Soldiers and Sailors Monument.

Little pilgrim—gone, perhaps removed

taken

by a local to an alleyway close by.

In his place, a bright spot of yellow satin
and thin blue shadow of the angel who
perches on top of the observation tower.

Indianapolis, October

Mantis

September, another falls loose,
knocked from late-blooming calendulas,
as I deadhead,
shake, gather, optimistically
scatter remaining seeds.

This delicate carnivore, gangly,
deep yellow-green, body swaying,
mimics a slight breeze,
small head cocked in deep thought.

Fluttering forelegs spike
my finger, attach like Velcro,
then release. I do not bleed.

I try to coax, remove it
so gently to another blade,
but a body part is lost.

I save a hinged leg
in a glass jar, watch colors fade,
the tiny exoskeleton emerge.

I slow down,
sit on the brick planter, soiled hands
folded. His image, so distant,
holds me like prey.

Naturally Religious

The small trilobite rests—
always a surprise
in this seldom-worn jacket.
I touch, feel forests generate
coal, hear the whack
of flying reptiles skirting a dying furnace,
the grind and rip,
new mountains forming.

On my bookshelf, the Ashanti god
sits on his stool
(a replica from the Smithsonian).
I see honor as he trades gold
for salt. I hear
temple bells initiate the first cry.

We wash saffron robes in the Ganges,
and the aborigine
completes the stone circle
uniting the world.
In the West, round pebbles travel
over ancient gravesites,
and the young prairie blooms fragrant,
air in its prime,
fish breath from an old sea floor!

We listen, measure, sharpen
the plow, sort recipes,
and rearrange tools in a red metal box.

Ship Burial

At the Sutton Hoo Exhibit, British Museum

I know what's caught inside—too much
to hold in a single day, or three, or four.

I never go in right away.
I even have time for a nap in the sun.

I will not read every catalog card.
I will not stop in the cafe and gift shops.

I will only see the ship burial:
the beds, golden dishes and chairs,

party artifacts—the table set,
goblets and hair combs placed just so.

It's most like a gravesite where one
would go to see if family headstones

have been disturbed, if plastic flowers
and metal cans lie strewn about.

But everything is the same, yet unearthed:
reverent, humble, asking for a blessing.

Leger

lair, couch, bed, lying, illness
leggerbed. (old Eng./Anglo-Saxon)

Remnants of a 7th century monastic order found
on the banks of the River Cam! Tombs
of young women unearthed, only one placed
in a burial bed complete with iron springs.

Were her trinkets odd, ordinary?
(I think not.)
Look at the rare pectoral cross stitched
to her gown, garnet studded brooch,
and iron belt, her chatelaine.

She is the only one placed among a robin's
delicate bones. The grave goods: a small purse
with glass beads and a single violet that says spring.
I imagine spindles spinning, chimes singing.

In earlier times this ground held a marsh,
no zephyr's sweet breath, but home to the pox
and poisonous berries mistaken for tender shoots
of yarrow and yew. And, like a pillow on a bed,
a pregnant bank swelled and overflowed.

Chaucer's Reeve lived right here, not knowing
what existed beneath. The River Cam
still lingers, watches the next layer begin.
And here I find her simple loom,
yarn still attached, weaving unfinished.

Stratigraphy

Platelets shift,
grind against a flat world, this poem drawn
in quadrants, points refracting,
jagged cells, trapezoids
mined deep as from
musty boxes in long-forgotten
clearinghouses.

The poet looks in other closets,
armoires—hidden words behind wood panels
papered in black *toile*—
scrapes deep crevices, taps a bit of shale,
wonders if every poem
has another shelf life?

Words, like delicate mica,
dislodge with pick, shatter—an uneasy puzzle
a therapist might direct a patient
to rearrange: eyes, nose,
        mouth in right order
or, like a marionette stretched too far,
the unarticulated skeleton: arms,
        legs, head snapping
back to edges that don't match. She
walks the escarpment; crushed
granite cracks underfoot.

High above the valley floor,
she notices a slit in the burned-out
rock shelter,
fragrant pollen dormant
for decades, sprouting new growth.

Poetry 101

A Cento

I am writing this poem on the back
of a grocery list. In the opening words this:
"Too many stars for our own good."

Empty places of the poem:
arms lopped, something dragged away:
the odor of the poem.

This is what I see in my dreams about final exams,
a bulletin from the poetry factory:
We like our images stuck on with morticians wax.

(You can't repeat this class in summer:
the course is only offered once.)

The truth is, none of my relatives writes poems.

A little poem, a sigh, at the cost
of indescribable losses:
fingerprints of the universe, maps you cannot read.

Clarity

How can I separate this confusion: fire from green?
Old alchemy dwindles and sets teeth on edge.

When a flame has gone green, the heart instinctively
knows, and rhythm shrinks to pulsing embers,

an afterglow of mustard and smoky tannins
all charcoal now, diminished to a new dust.

A cloudy film mixes with remnants of conversation—
too distant for clarity to identify its touch, its heart.

Silhouettes of pine trees edge the horizon. Someone
with scissors cuts away the sky, leaving sharp points

in the blackened forest. White arcs on a quarter moon.
My nail traces chartreuse light, the edge of healing.

Wintering

In October, writing a bear poem,
I think about my own hibernation.

Wild apples fallen deep
in abandoned fields give off cider.

Squirrels chew and scatter
maple's ivory seeds.

The she-bear nestles in, carries
sperm that don't impregnate

but temporarily float
in wintering fluids,

a rich ovum bath, so cubs
appear after the spring thaw.

I look forward to January,
my bed piled with books,

resisting fog and cold,
the kernel planted—the husk firm.

IV.

Trilobite

For years I carried a trilobite
in my jacket pocket.
Sometimes during lecture,
I pulled it out, dime-sized,
like a thumbprint
with ridges and backbones.
Reduction of larger-celled animals,
I never thought of it as a totem
that is more often a deer,
snake, bear, or other archaic symbol.
Smaller than a butter pat,
fine-tuned exoskeleton,
down to basics, dense in its grayness,
a darker storm cloud, once-living
spines pricking wakefulness,
too much energy for meditation.
Off the subject, I see lines
leave my students' faces
as they relax back into childhood.
Rather than continue
our discussion of personality
theory, neurons and obsessions,
they brainstorm their own
talismans: bottle caps,
baseball cards,
shells from the coast—
small pleasures in small things.

Full of Sighs

This is my life: crystal dew, sun's
temporary passing, apricot orchards, fruit
soon overripe. On Interstate 5,
I pull north near the Coast Range
enveloped in a strong scent of pet bear.
From an oak forest, the green man
emerges. I have fantasized
his bristles, felt wrapped
in the blue-blown faces of his bindweed.
How fetching the bit of beaver fat
in his beard, brown berry eyes flecked
gold, a slow swagger, a smolder about him.
He straggles in, holds a crust of bread,
winks a hint of brandy and toads.
On his back, a rage of scars.
I bask in his vermillion coals,
juniper pods so old they've turned to gin.
I don't care how decrepit—
myths are hard work!
Just for a moment he gives
me a break from rubber and asphalt.
Foothills gleam orchid, twilight
softens vastness. Sharp edges of the interstate
push day into night, the Pacific
full of sighs: waves waffle
in black, endless, undulating weaves.

Forecast: the sea, calm and rippled.
This is my life.

A Bar in the Tropics

Parrot green kudzu vines tug,
unleash chipped railings.
Wild grapes crush wads
of white plastic shopping bags.

On the wobbly veranda,
caught beneath floorboards,
a tattered calendar, worn
ephemera, only three pages

remaining: a temple
strung with opaque lanterns,
a bleeding heart some
might call valentine

and the only printed page,
a cartoon for happy hour
featuring the "Mud Slide."

Is this the holy libation?
The last tenement standing?
The new world order?

Three Glasses of Wine

At the first cup, man drinks wine
at the second, wine drinks wine
at the third, wine drinks man.
—Japanese Proverb

The first glass,
I think of all I must do,
the poem I intend to write,
the meter I cannot memorize.

The second glass,
how red the red! Sparks
when held to the sun,
santé de Cristo.
A slight spill resembles
the west coast of Africa.

The third,
I could copy Chaucer
and his gift of the French lyric.
A spot coagulates purple,
resembles the lost continent of Mu.

*****

Postscript: I review my illegible notes
splashed with the brown stain
of forgotten countries.

Manhattan

For Greg

Evening, early January,
the drink deep and straight up,
        dinner with this person
so close to me for 30 years.

Slow sips while we anticipate
menu selections: prime rib, lobster,
fisherman's platter?

We enjoy the privacy of dark booths,
tables laminated with nautical maps and coins,
other twosomes, faces
in the glow of cell phones.

        A slow start to the day,
two hours in bed with the *Chronicle,* considering
the annual white sales.
Time spent on nothing, really: the last
wreath and bell stored away,
remembering children who came caroling on the 26th,

        "To make the season last," they said.

        Over creamy chowder,
I look up to a painting of a dog in a sailor suit,
smoking a pipe, and another
of Johnny Depp as Jack Sparrow.

Some wouldn't consider this place romantic—
just a throwback.
        You like sweets.
I give you the maraschino.

Sparkling Moscato, Schmooze Time

The artist was an isolated character,
his contact with the public minimal and rare.
Thank God, when a collector gave them the few francs
for a *poulet au pot, a gâteau,* to pay a model
or rent the atelier.

Proverbs are part of the language, spice
and shortcut, commonplace banalities, closer to the truth:

    lambs once counted, the wolf eats them

    to put one's head in the wolf's jaw
    one would have to rent rooms in one's head

    who would mow an egg?

    who would take the moon with one's teeth?

Pour rien, is dirt cheap
Pour rire, is to laugh
Infidel, unfaithful
An artist's *métier* is his craft.
Frequently he lives on *bouille de maïs*

Ironically, every conversation is peppered
with *D'accord.* Agreed.

Poem for a Happy Place

A Cento

All my life I have been restless. I have felt
there is something more wonderful than glass.

Anyone who comes must travel slowly with
thoughts through the soft rain, like mist and mica.

With a blue rag, in the women's restroom in Singapore,
she is washing airport ashtrays big as hubcaps.

I want her to rise up from the slop and fly
down the river. Her smile was only for my sake.

We stepped from the car to the garden, where tea
was brought among the unforgotten flowers, and

let the white cups cool before we raised them to our lips.
For hours, I picked wildflowers from the grass, blue stars

on long green stems in my trembling hands; they glistened
like fire. A person wants to stand in a happy place in a poem.

Think how somewhere in Tuscany a small spider might
even now be stepping forth, maybe singing a tiny song.

Once in a while, you creep out of your own life, an explosion,
imagination! I am willing to be that long blue body of light.

He looked into the faces of that frightened crowd.
I am that wild darkness...that happy place in a poem.

A Paris Reading at the End of the Occupation

After Simone de Beauvoir

A reading of Picasso's play, *Desire Caught
by the Tail,* hosted by an Argentine millionaire.

We had to amuse ourselves somehow. Even crosswords
were banned; they might pass on secret codes.

All parts were taken—Big Foot, Thin Misery, The Tart—
applauded by Sartre and Camus with great enthusiasm.

Picasso brought an elegant *chocolate gâteau.*
Someone pointed out a gorgeous man...Georges Braque.

I fussed over what to wear; to Picasso's delight,
borrowed a red angora sweater and big blue pearls.

Our hosts kept us past curfew. We stayed the night.
It was premature gaiety. The city had become

a vast gloomy Stalag, but a sense of freedom
hung about avenues, monuments, prisoners' barracks.

We heard the Allies reached Italy; Rome was
next. All over Paris, drawings of a snail

appeared crawling up the Italian coastline
in English and American national colors.

There was enough wine left for more scenes. In
darkness, we tasted victory, a stealthy pleasure.

And morning, a good time to be out, once again
greeted by the warmth of fresh yeasty bread.

Valley Oaks

She was a dutiful daughter, read Simone de Beauvoir.
Now she rocks, knees thumping out rhythms

on the old treadle machine, impairment of simple
thoughts riding in a blue Buick, blithely rumbling past

heritage oaks that defy auditory attempts to track
subterranean movement. Beautiful machinery, these humans

and oaks, fifty organic chemicals, all the same pattern,
nature's tendrils reaching too far for plaque to shock,

surprise, disrupt switches. But her tough fibers
are indifferent, new categories destroyed every day.

Few clicks, little sound; tugs and scar tissue here and
there erase fleeting memories. Now, evening branches

burrow under her blanket. She knows bright red apples
but not the jagged jaw of the son who brings them.

Only the night nurse dares shake her in time for supper.

Prufrock in Uenice

No one will take our photo in the piazza
     as we enjoy a strong espresso

or coming out of the cathedral
trying to decide if we should risk
     a boat ride to Murano Island.

We try not to look like tourists
but your shirt, a blue line print on parchment
with its ancient map of the world, draws stares.

We are not royalty; no one expects
     anything from us.

We purchase toy gondolas for the holiday
tree we haven't put up in years.

The movement of the city is gentle; we can hear
floorboards meet that gently grind and squeak.

Our suitcase wears thin.
The zipper looses stitching.
The duct tape inside might show—
     what if we're searched?

Better to die, even drown, near famous museums
     and not know the embarrassment.

We do enjoy the *Prosecco* and small pastries.
We do love the pink peaches reflecting dawn.

Aquatics

I keep a low profile
because I have another life.
Sure, I'm proud
of my physique,
aging and ravaged as it is.
My tongue is foreign;
I don't speak,
just lie in water, a sleek seal.
Younger women don't
look my way.
Yet another, older and pale,
I'm certain she watches me,
doesn't understand
culture, the evil eye!
Am I looking at her?
An even flow,
measured buoyancy,
she asks some silly
question about water wings.
Everything is evidence.
I'm not leaving.
My body has questions.
It will be a long summer.
        "Touch me,
touch my coppery skin."

Leaving Ella

On summer nights, Dad drove around the city
while the house cooled.
Windows rolled down in the old Buick, we licked
the last of our pineapple sherbet.
He turned up side streets with small bars.
Front doors opened
to the sound of jazz in a blue Chesterfield haze,
summer jazz, maybe a sax
or a single low horn in no hurry,
notes muffled
        like a grown-up lullaby.

No surprise my first record purchase—
Ella's *Tea Leaves,* her bouncy version:
sparks of Romany fires and golden earrings.

We packed for the move west. "Records are too fragile!"
At our basement sale, Ella lay on the table
next to Mother's carnival glass.
Grief stayed all through St. Louis, Gallup,
Tucson and Blythe (the border crossing).

Eventually, I dated a bass player
in the high school combo.
Ella sang on the Perry Como Show, older than I imagined.
There were trips to the Hollywood Bowl
featuring George Shearing
and progressive trios at the Hat and Cane Supper Club.

Tonight it's warm in the Valley.
I could be enjoying the scent of new orange groves,
yet it's the old blue notes that satisfy,
the back streets and Dad driving us into dreaming.

Pillow Words

In the Japanese style: makurakotoba

Over the Coast Range
rough-cut seas exist, a *mirume*-filled bay,
    pencil-slim steeple on the bluff.

Here in low hills, a hawk's snow-dusted feather
lands on a fog-splintered railing.
    I hold my silent-mug of tea.

White-frothed spill bubbles above the creek
where maple seeds spin white.

A canopy of pines startles me,
    bower-green candles quake
like sectioned harlequins. One tree, to the side
    —an origami, wrinkled into itself.

I finger my old robe, elegant flat-fell seams
    that never fray.

Soon, I take the bone-dry pill, lie
on my tear-sodden pillow, misshapen and wet,

and watch the last purple-veined berry leaves,
spotted and waxy, crawl up the lintel.

I think of warmer days,
    nodding narrow-needle grass
(*Nassella cernua*) and golden-cheeked elderberry.

We gathered armfuls and cooked
yellow blossoms in our butter-creamed omelets.

They're coming tomorrow, want me
to sell, but I've made up my love-soaked mind!

"I won't sign anything until...
    I talk to the temple-smashing prophet!"

In one soft click, the arched-branched maple changes
to bright scarlet, like the soft-clip of a child's barrette.

Home Again

Time works its cure,
like a few surgeries, or mice
eating away the rice,
and glitter from your wedding cards—
a long way, whether it's miles or memory.
I stopped, walked around.
Old sleeping bags
slumped against boarded windows
and a crack house stood next door.
After four years, new dual panes
and a glassed-in porch shone
like a beacon. I peeked
into the living room where the baby
grand stood, the windows where we hung
paper curtains—the empty space
where rugs were rolled back on Saturday nights,
the empty space for polkas and fox-trots.
The crack house is still next door
but, on my doorstep, a child's toy cup,
milky green glass, and a tiny hole—
for even the smallest finger.

Sunday

If I pay attention, this day will slow.
I won't look back from a darkened sky
and regret what wasn't done.
The wind comes, the warm stillness
of yesterday gone in this early spring.

My bouquet of yellow iris
is vibrant after a week, not one fallen petal
on the starched linen cloth.

The only thing I vow to do today
is clip coupons, check the new perennials
for dry spots, make a simple stew.
Too much of life I've spent on pledges,
the disquiet of how to fill these twelve hours.

Like the child who thinks the sun
is following her, I place my foot down
against advancing shadows
and reflect on another time
when threshers went home early.
We sat until the coffee pot emptied,
then our family returned
to the richness of that other Sunday.

Bungalow

How can I forget our small gray bungalow
where in summer we sat late,
gazed from the porch at the rusted garden sculptures

where star man and dancer, with bird on toe,
flaunted their lust
at the edge of the dry streambed?

Mornings, the late stars,
a wash of chandeliers still bright on windowpanes,

a smattering of tiny planets retreating into a yellow sky.

We pulled back the heavy maroon draperies
splashed with white cabbage roses,

then roused to coffee, toast, and the chatter of jays.

Two jams open at the same time—
one berry and one peach.

The Magpie

—Claude Monet

There is vintage light in these snow-dropped fields
of Normandy where winter writes the architecture of summer:

gate, fence, trees, house, all hinged to fallow fields,
a landscape waiting. Trees tilt left, shadows bend right,

a net of deciduous limbs punctuates the chalky sky.
One person left early; footsteps sunk in mauve depressions

glaze over in afternoon's blue chill. A full day for this most
sociable of birds; now she only wants silence.

Her nest, not far away, wraps snug in mistletoe.
Cold fluffs the smallish body. One eye on the post,

she remembers the strip of red meat left yesterday.
Does she remember summer, the path strewn with kernels?

Pie, the only deep hue, the dusk of your chest, struck
by a small patch of flecked sun. Now late, your shape

dissolves into the nearest footstep. You are the dwindling sun,
the windblown star. On your top rung, rest quiet, crow dark.

Notes

"Catching the Last Metro." After Simone de Bouvier, *Memoirs of a Dutiful Daughter* (Harper Colophon Books, 1959).

"Declaration." A prompt by Molly Fisk, from the movie, *Bull Durham.*

"Hoarfrost." Critic, Jules Antoine Castagnary in *Le Siècle:* "Pissarro commits the grave error of painting fields with shadows cast by trees placed outside the frame. The viewer is left to suppose they exist."

"My Kitchen in California." Recipe cited: "Marseille's Candlemas Cookies," Richard Olney, *Simple French Cooking* (Wiley Publishing, Inc., 1992).

"False Pilgrim." One who hires another to go on pilgrimage.

"Imprint." After "Nostros," Louise Glück.

"Limberlost." The home of author Gene Stratton Porter in northern Indiana.

"The Celadon Bird." Some lines after reading Emily D and Elizabeth B.

"Poetry 101." Ruth Stone: "Theology," "Body Among Trees," "Orange Poem Praising Brown," "Flash," "This Space." Wislawa Szymborska: "Evaluation of an Unwritten Poem," "Brueghel's Two Monkeys," "Nothing Twice," "In Praise of my Sister," "A Large Number."

"Sparkling Moscato, Schmooze Time." Found poem: *Depths of Glory* (about Camille Pissarro) (Irving Stone, 1985, from the Glossary).

"Poem for a Happy Place." Mary Oliver, *New and Selected Poems* (Beacon Press, 1992): "Whelks," "Marengo," "Singapore," "Alligator Poem," "Three Poems for James Wright," "Acid," "The Buddha's Last Instruction."

"A Paris Reading." After Simone de Bouvier, *The Prime of Life* (Harper Colophon Books, 1962).

"Bungalow." After Baudelaire's poem, "I Have Not Forgotten."

Acknowledgments

Grateful acknowledgment is made to the editors of the following publications in which these works or earlier versions previously appeared:

Adanna Literary Journal: "Leger"
Alehouse: "Ship Burial"
Arsenic Lobster Poetry Journal: "False Pilgrim"
Black Poppy: "Omen"
Centrifugal Eye: "Bungalow"
Clackamas Literary Review: "Oblique," "A Paris Reading"
Clare Literary Journal: "All Degrees of White"
Coal Hill Review: "Our Room with Open Door"
Colere: "Sparkling Moscato, Schmooze Time"
Convergence: "Snowshoe in Summer," "Poetry 101"
Cosumnes River Journal: "Pillow Words"
Earth's Daughters: "Wild Asparagus"
Edge: "House Special," "Main Street," "Pilgrim State"
Ekphrasis: "Hoarfrost," "Canyon with Crows"
Forge Poetry Journal: "Gremlin"
Gertrude: "Acorn"
Grasslimb: "Poem for a Happy Place," "Aquatics"
Life and Legends: "Hermosa Beach"
Medusas Kitchen: "Cartographer"
North Dakota Quarterly: "Wintering," "The Magpie"
Ophidian: "Sugarloaf," "Declaration"
Pearl: "Day Moon Watching"
Penumbra: "Reading a Used Book in July"
Perfume River Poetry Review: "My Kitchen in California"
Poesy: "Clarity"
Poetic Matrix: "First Love"
Poetry Depth Quarterly: "Invisible"
Poppy Road Review: "Moonlight"
The Ravens Perch: "Mind of the Glacier"
Red Poppy: "Three Wines"
Ruah: "Mantis"
South Dakota Review: "Sifting," "V Shapes Against Blue"
Squaw Valley Review: "November 2 A.M.," "Full of Sighs"
Suisun Valley Review: "A Bar in the Tropics"

Sun, Shadow Mountain Anthology: "Naturally Religious"
Tahoe Blues Anthology: "Three about Ecstasy"
The Gathering: "Prufrock in Venice"
Tiger's Eye Journal: "Rabbits," "Mother Mary"
Tipton Poetry Journal: "Home Again," "Leaving Ella"
Valparaiso Poetry Journal: "A Date at the La Brea Tar Pits," "Sunday"
Verse Wisconsin: "Weekly Reader"
Willard and Maple: "Limberlost"
Winter Rising: "Imprint"
WTF: "Black Figs"

The following poems were previously published in chapbooks:
"Catching the Last Metro," *Women in Cafes* (Finishing Line Press, 2012);
"The Keeping Room," *The Keeping Room* (Rattlesnake Press, 2005);
"Stratigraphy," *The Meaning of Monoliths* (Poet's Corner Press, 2006);
"Dungeness," "The Celadon Bird" and "Manhattan," *Brief Immensity*
(Finishing Line Press, 2017).

"Imprint," part of a group of poems, won First Prize in the 2015 Winter
in Variations Contest (sponsored by Bill Holm Witness Poetry).

Thank you to Diane Kistner and FutureCycle Press for appreciating
Limberlost, and for all phases of its production.

Much appreciation to the editors of *Ekphrasis* for nominating "Canyon
with Crows," and the editors of Finishing Line Press for nominating
"V Shapes Against Blue," for a Pushcart Prize.

Special thanks to the Community of Writers at Squaw Valley, especially
Sharon Olds and C. D. Wright who advised on first drafts of some poems.
I am also grateful to Kim Addonizio from the Mendocino Coast Writer's
Conference and Dana Levin, the Tomales Bay Writer's Workshop, as well
as local poets who offered suggestions: Andrea Ross, Rae Gouirand,
Rebecca Morrison, Alexa Mergen, Colette Jonopulos and Kim Wyatt.

My gratitude to Russell Thorburn, Tom Goff and Greg Chalpin, all
instrumental in assisting with sequencing, editing and formatting of
the manuscript.

About FutureCycle Press

FutureCycle Press is dedicated to publishing lasting English-language poetry books, chapbooks, and anthologies in both print-on-demand and Kindle ebook formats. Founded in 2007 by long-time independent editor/publishers and partners Diane Kistner and Robert S. King, the press incorporated as a nonprofit in 2012. A number of our editors are distinguished poets and writers in their own right, and we have been actively involved in the small press movement going back to the early seventies.

The FutureCycle Poetry Book Prize and honorarium is awarded annually for the best full-length volume of poetry we publish in a calendar year. Introduced in 2013, our Good Works projects are anthologies devoted to issues of universal significance, with all proceeds donated to a related worthy cause. Our Selected Poems series highlights contemporary poets with a substantial body of work to their credit; with this series we strive to resurrect work that has had limited distribution and is now out of print.

We are dedicated to giving all of the authors we publish the care their work deserves, making our catalog of titles the most diverse and distinguished it can be, and paying forward any earnings to fund more great books.

We've learned a few things about independent publishing over the years. We've also evolved a unique, resilient publishing model that allows us to focus mainly on vetting and preserving for posterity poetry collections of exceptional quality without becoming overwhelmed with bookkeeping and mailing, fundraising activities, or taxing editorial and production "bubbles." To find out more about what we are doing, come see us at www.futurecycle.org.

The FutureCycle Poetry Book Prize

All full-length volumes of poetry published by FutureCycle Press in a given calendar year are considered for the annual FutureCycle Poetry Book Prize. This allows us to consider each submission on its own merits, outside of the context of a contest. Too, the judges see the finished book, which will have benefitted from the beautiful book design and strong editorial gloss we are famous for.

The book ranked the best in judging is announced as the prizewinner in the subsequent year. There is no fixed monetary award; instead, the winning poet receives an honorarium of 20% of the total net royalties from all poetry books and chapbooks the press sold online in the year the winning book was published. The winner is also accorded the honor of being on the panel of judges for the next year's competition; all judges receive copies of all contending books to keep for their personal library.

www.ingramcontent.com/pod-product-compliance
Lightning Source LLC
Chambersburg PA
CBHW070003100426
42741CB00012B/3109